A New True Book

HURRICANES

By Arlene Erlbach

CHILDRENS PRESS®
CHICAGO

Boats washed ashore by Hurricane
Andrew, which struck Florida and
Louisiana in August 1992

PHOTO CREDITS

AP/Wide World Photos—2, 5 (2 photos), 7, 16, 20,
21 (top and bottom right), 27, 28, 32 (2 photos), 45
(left)

Knight-Ridder/Tribune Graphics Network—33

Courtesy of National Weather Service—26 (2
photos)

Photri—Cover Inset, 11, 22, 24, 29, 40

Reuters/Bettmann Newsphotos—45 (right)

Tony Stone, Worldwide/Chicago—© Wynn Miller,
Cover; © Jim Pickerell, 21 (bottom left)

SuperStock International, Inc.—31; © C. Harris,
15; © A. Upitis, 35; © H. Lambert, 39; © K. Moan, 42

UPI/Bettmann Newsphotos—6 (left), 8, 25

Valan—© Chris Malazdrewicz, 6 (right); © J. R.
Page, 12

Art by Tom Dunnington—9, 13, 14, 36

Cover—Sea storm

Cover Inset—Apollo 9 view of cyclonic storm

Dedicated to Salo and Ilse Erlbach who weathered Andrew.

Library of Congress Cataloging-in-Publication Data

Erlbach, Arlene.
    Hurricanes / by Arlene Erlbach.
        p.   cm. — (A New true book)
    Includes index.
    Summary: Describes the movements and destructive
power of hurricanes and explains how they are
predicted and monitored.
    ISBN 0-516-01333-5
    1. Hurricanes—Juvenile literature.
[1. Hurricanes.] I. Title.
QC944.E75   1993
551.55′2—dc20   92-37811
                                         CIP
                                          AC

TABLE OF CONTENTS

WIND AND STORMS

The Earth is surrounded by a layer of air called the atmosphere. This air is warmed by the Sun.

As the warmed air rises, cooler air rushes in to take its place. This movement of air causes wind. The speed of the wind depends on how fast the air is moving.

If the air moves slowly, we

People fighting the hurricane winds and rain of Typhoon Luke
in Tokyo (left) and Hurricane Andrew in Louisiana (right)

feel a soft breeze. If the air
moves quickly, we feel a
strong wind blowing.

Sometimes wind blows
very fast. Rain or snow may
fall, too. Then we have a
storm.

5

Trees bend before the strong winds of a typhoon in Hawaii.
People on the island of Nassau in the Bahamas (inset)
caught in the winds of Hurricane Betsy in 1965

When rain falls and the wind blows more than 74 miles per hour, we have a powerful storm called a hurricane.

Hurricanes are the biggest and most dangerous storms on Earth.

The hurricane's wind blows rain sideways. It shatters windows and sometimes flattens houses. Trees are uprooted; cars are overturned. Hurricane winds can force ocean waves onto land. Rivers and lakes overflow. Sometimes cities and towns are flooded.

A water tower stands amid the destruction caused by Hurricane Andrew at Florida City, Florida, in August 1992.

The hurricanes that hit the Western Hemisphere usually begin in the warm waters off the west coast of Africa. Sometimes they start in the Caribbean Sea or the Gulf of Mexico.

Hurricanes usually form in July, August, or September.

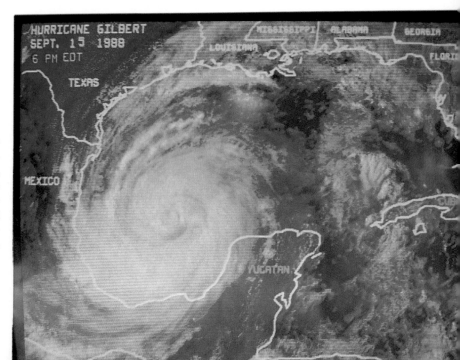

This satellite photo shows the huge, swirling clouds of Hurricane Gilbert heading north toward Texas in 1988.

HOW HURRICANES START

Hurricanes are enormous masses of whirling clouds. To understand how hurricanes start, we must know how these thunderclouds form.

Near the equator, the sun beats down on the oceans. This warms the waters, and

The equator is an imaginary line that goes around the Earth halfway between the North Pole and the South Pole.

EQUATOR

Sun

causes some of the ocean water to evaporate. This warm, damp air rises and cools in the atmosphere. Then the air condenses–it changes into tiny water drops. The condensed air forms clouds.

Clouds are huge masses of water vapor. They contain billions of drops of water and zillions of water molecules.

Cumulus clouds are white and fluffy.

At first, the clouds are fluffy, white cumulus clouds. If their water drops get too heavy, they fall to Earth as rain. But sometimes, warm air rising over the ocean makes the cumulus clouds grow. Then they turn into

Dark gray cumulonimbus clouds produce thunderstorms.

cumulonimbus clouds.
These big, dark clouds
produce thunderstorms.

Wind blows these clouds
west over the ocean. The
warm ocean water keeps
evaporating and more warm,
damp air rises. The
thunderclouds grow larger

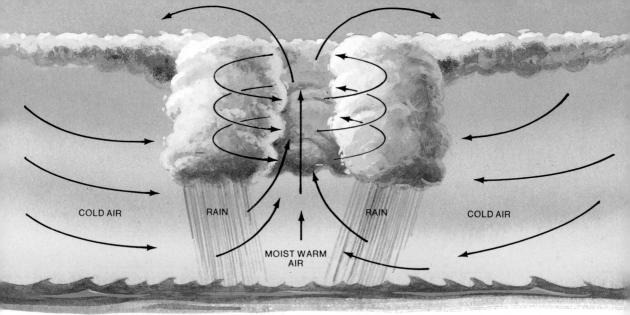

COLD AIR   RAIN   RAIN   COLD AIR

MOIST WARM AIR

As warm, moist air rises, cold air rushes in to replace it. This causes winds to blow.

and more clouds form. This large cluster of clouds is called an easterly wave.

Sometimes an easterly wave breaks up and becomes a thunderstorm. But sometimes it picks up more clouds and grows into a tropical disturbance.

13

FROM TROPICAL DISTURBANCE TO TROPICAL STORM

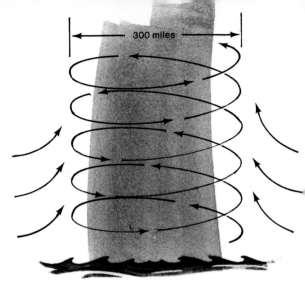

300 miles

A tropical depression, or tropical storm, can cover more than 300 miles.

If the tropical disturbance does not break up, it collects more clouds. As this storm grows, its winds cause the clouds to whip around in a giant circle.

When the clouds begin to spin, the cloud mass is called a tropical depression. It is getting closer to becoming a hurricane.

The tropical depression may break up and come down as a thunderstorm. If not, it moves over the ocean, picking up more water vapor. Its winds whirl faster. When the winds spin faster than 39 miles per hour, the tropical depression

Hurricanes and tropical storms are especially dangerous near the shoreline. Violent winds and high ocean waves cause heavy damage.

Meteorologists use radar and computers to track dangerous storms.

becomes a tropical storm. If this violent storm hits land, it can cause floods and blow down houses and trees.

Weather scientists called meteorologists watch tropical storms closely. About half of all tropical storms turn into hurricanes.

FROM TROPICAL STORM TO HURRICANE

Many tropical storms die at sea. They never reach land. But some grow stronger as they move over the ocean.

As more water vapor is sucked into the clouds, the winds increase. When the winds move faster than 74 miles per hour, the storm has become a hurricane. And it is still growing!

As the hurricane moves over warm water, it picks up more warm air. The winds blow faster and faster. The winds of a severe hurricane can reach speeds of 175 miles per hour or more. And the whirling mass of clouds can cover thousands of miles.

Many hurricanes come down over ocean water and do no harm. But some hurricanes strike land. Then the hurricane destroys huge areas and causes great human suffering.

WORST HURRICANES IN OR NEAR THE U.S.

Some hurricanes don't have names because the weather service didn't officially name them until 1950.

Year	Name	Location	Number of Deaths
1900		Galveston, Texas	About 6,000 (the deadliest storm ever to hit the U.S.)
1928		Puerto Rico Florida	2,136 deaths (1,836 dead in Florida)
1979	David	Guadeloupe Martinique Dominica Dominican Republic	1,100 (raked U.S. coast, killing 16)
1919		Florida Texas	800 (300 in Florida and 500 in Texas)
1938		New England	600 dead
1944	Great Atlantic Hurricane	Northeastern United States	600 dead
1935	The Labor Day Hurricane	Florida Keys	408 (winds over 200 miles per hour)
1957	Audrey	Texas Louisiana coast	390
1909		Mississippi Louisiana	350
1969	Camille	Mississippi West Virginia Virginia	256 (winds over 200 miles per hour)
1980	Allen	Caribbean Islands & Texas	250 dead in Caribbean Islands. (the worst Caribbean storm ever recorded)
1955	Diane	Northeastern United States	184

Fortunately, hurricanes weaken after they hit land. They lose power when they no longer have the ocean water to make them grow. But before the hurricane dies, it does enormous damage.

Hurricane damage in Providence, Rhode Island, in 1938. A storm surge drove the boat onshore and covered the cars with thirteen feet of water.

Paths of destruction: A Jamaican woman (top) tries to clear her porch of debris left by a hurricane. Cars crushed by trees (bottom left) and small airplanes (bottom right) destroyed on the ground by violent winds are common sights after a hurricane.

This photograph, made by an Apollo spaceship in Earth orbit, clearly shows the circular pattern of clouds in a hurricane.

THE STORM WITH AN EYE

Satellite cameras have photographed hurricanes. These pictures show masses of clouds whirling around a quiet area in the center of the storm. This calm area is called the eye of the hurricane.

In the eye, the winds are calm, and the sun shines through.

But in the wall clouds surrounding the eye, the winds whirl the fastest (200 miles per hour or more). They produce the heaviest rain and do the most damage.

When the eye is passing over an area, the hurricane seems to stop. But soon the rest of the hurricane hits with the same dreadful force.

Flooding causes heavy damage in hurricanes. The water from storm surges or from rivers and streams swollen by the heavy rains can invade cities and towns.

HOW HURRICANES DESTROY

The rain and wind of a hurricane are powerful. The rain causes floods. The wind smashes everything in its path. But the most dangerous force in a hurricane is its storm surge. This happens

Huge waves pound a beachfront hotel in St. Augustine, Florida, during Hurricane Dora in 1964.

when hurricane winds cause ocean waves to rise and roll across land. These waves can reach a height of thirty feet.

A storm surge moves quickly. Most deaths in hurricanes are caused by storm surges.

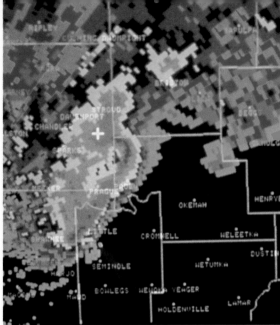

With the National Weather Service radar, called NEXRAD, meteorologists can "see" inside storms to track them in their early stages. Each NEXRAD has a work station (left), where operators display the storm data (right) on a map.

PREDICTING HURRICANES

Nobody can stop a hurricane, but meteorologists can predict them. They can tell people when and where a hurricane will strike.

Scientists at the National

26

Meteorologists at the National Hurricane Center in Florida study information on a storm that may become a dangerous hurricane.

Hurricane Center in Miami, Florida, track hurricanes on radar. The hurricane season lasts from June through November, but these scientists watch storms all year round.

This artist's drawing shows a weather satellite that was put into orbit around the Earth to study weather patterns.

Weather satellites photograph tropical depressions and tropical storms. Meteorologists study these pictures. Often, they can tell if a storm will become a hurricane.

Sometimes scientists fly planes right into the eye of

the hurricane. Instruments in the plane record wind speed and direction. Other instruments measure the amount of water in the clouds.

Scientists use this information to predict the force and the path of the hurricane. They can tell if it will hit land or not.

Scientists fly special airplanes into hurricanes to measure and record wind speed and direction.

HOW STRONG ARE HURRICANES?

Hurricanes are classified by their wind speed. They are measured on a scale of 1 to 5:

Category 1   74 to 95 miles per hour
Category 2   96 to 110 miles per hour
Category 3   111 to 130 miles per hour
Category 4   131 to 155 miles per hour
Category 5   more than 155 miles per hour

The greater the wind speed, the greater is the destruction. Category 1 hurricanes break off tree branches and blow down power lines. Category 5

hurricanes destroy buildings—
and even entire towns.

In recent times, only two
category 5 hurricanes have
hit the United States. One
struck Tampa, Florida, in
1935. The other one—
Hurricane Camille—hit seven
states in 1969.

Hurricane
Camille left
this trail of
destruction
in Mississippi
in 1969.

Homestead, Florida, was ruined by Hurricane Andrew. A survivor (left) surveys the damage, while a department-store dummy (right) lies in broken glass.

But a category 4 hurricane is also very powerful. Hurricane Andrew in 1992 was a category 4 storm. It destroyed more than 60,000 houses and cost more than 30 billion dollars in damage. Over thirty people lost their lives.

Measuring a hurricane's strength

Hurricane Andrew came ashore in Florida Monday as a Category 4 hurricane. Only two Category 5 storms have hit the United States since record-keeping began: the 1935 Labor Day hurricane in the Florida Keys and Hurricane Camille along the Mississippi coast in 1969. The five classes of hurricanes:

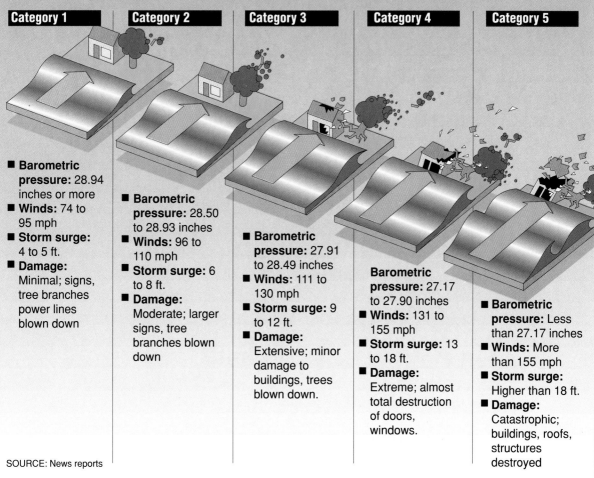

Category 1

- **Barometric pressure:** 28.94 inches or more
- **Winds:** 74 to 95 mph
- **Storm surge:** 4 to 5 ft.
- **Damage:** Minimal; signs, tree branches power lines blown down

Category 2

- **Barometric pressure:** 28.50 to 28.93 inches
- **Winds:** 96 to 110 mph
- **Storm surge:** 6 to 8 ft.
- **Damage:** Moderate; larger signs, tree branches blown down

Category 3

- **Barometric pressure:** 27.91 to 28.49 inches
- **Winds:** 111 to 130 mph
- **Storm surge:** 9 to 12 ft.
- **Damage:** Extensive; minor damage to buildings, trees blown down.

Category 4

- **Barometric pressure:** 27.17 to 27.90 inches
- **Winds:** 131 to 155 mph
- **Storm surge:** 13 to 18 ft.
- **Damage:** Extreme; almost total destruction of doors, windows.

Category 5

- **Barometric pressure:** Less than 27.17 inches
- **Winds:** More than 155 mph
- **Storm surge:** Higher than 18 ft.
- **Damage:** Catastrophic; buildings, roofs, structures destroyed

SOURCE: News reports

8/24/92

Knight-Ridder Tribune/JEFF DIONISE

NAMING HURRICANES

Our word *hurricane* comes from the name Hurakán. The people of Central America believed Hurakán was a god that caused storms.

Each hurricane is given a name by a committee of meteorologists. They choose the name from an alphabetical list of male and

Electrical workers in New York repair power
lines downed by a hurricane.

female names. The first
hurricane of the year gets a
name that starts with an A.
The next gets a name that
starts with B, and so on. The
list alternates between male
and female names. It has no
names starting with the
letters Q, U, X, Y, or Z. **35**

Fortunately, the scientists have never needed to use all 21 names.

In other parts of the world people call hurricanes by different names. Australian people call them Willy Willies. They're called cyclones in India. In China, people refer to them as typhoons. Filipinos call them Bagios.

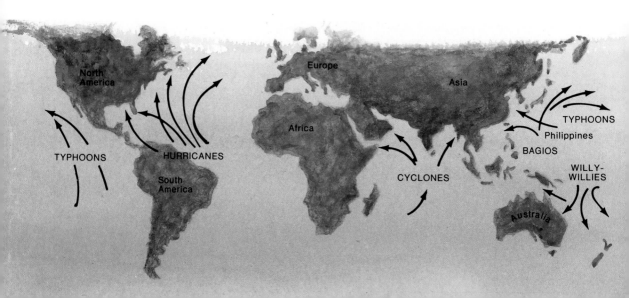

MAJOR HURRICANES, TYPHOONS, AND CYCLONES WORLDWIDE

Type of Storm	Year	Location	Number of Deaths
Cyclone	1970	Bangladesh	At least 500,000 killed (the absolute worst storm ever)
Typhoon	1881	Indochina	300,000
Cyclone	1876	India	200,000
Cyclone	1882	India	100,000
Cyclone	1864	India	70,000
Cyclone	1942	India	40,000
Cyclone	1965	Bangladesh	25,000
Cyclone	1963	Bangladesh	22,000
Double Cyclones	October 10, 1960 October 31, 1960	Bangladesh	14,000
Cyclone	1965	Bangladesh	13,000
Typhoon	1906	Hong Kong	10,000
Hurricane	1703	England	8,000
Hurricane	1900	Galveston, Texas	At least 6,000 (the worst natural disaster in U.S. history)

HURRICANES AND TORNADOES

Hurricanes are more destructive than tornadoes. A hurricane can cover hundreds of miles and last for days. Tornadoes usually cover less than a mile and last less than an hour.

Sometimes hurricanes cause tornadoes. Clouds and wind break away from hurricanes and become

A tornado touches down. Dark, greenish clouds
are a common sign that a tornado is near.

violent thunderstorms. Winds
inside these thunderstorms
form spinning, funnel-shaped
tornado clouds. Wind speed

Tornado touchdown at Tracy, Minnesota, on June 20, 1968

inside the tornado reaches 200 miles per hour.

Tornadoes don't include rain.

Hurricanes that happen thousands of miles away can affect our weather. Some of the clouds from the hurricane can break off and carry severe storms to where you live.

WATCHES AND WARNINGS

People are warned about hurricanes in the newspapers and on TV and radio. Regular programs are often interrupted to tell people about incoming storms.

Everyone should understand storm warnings and know what they mean.

Tropical Storm Warning:

A violent thunderstorm is on its way. It is probably best to

These low, dark clouds mean that a severe storm may be forming.

stay inside. Everything in your yard should be put away or covered. If you must leave your home, close all windows and bring pets indoors.

Hurricane Watch:

A hurricane might hit your area within 48 hours. Make sure your family has emergency supplies such as medicine, food, and water. Check your flashlight batteries because electricity may go out. Fill the car with gas. You may need to leave the area if the hurricane watch turns into a warning.

Hurricane Warning:

A hurricane will hit your area within 24 hours. It may be time to leave the area, especially if you live near a coastline.

These early warning messages save lives. Because scientists can predict the path of hurricanes, people have time to take shelter or leave the area.

A row of power lines torn down by Hurricane Hugo in Puerto Rico. After a hurricane passes, buildings look as if they have been ripped apart by an explosion (inset).

Today, although hurricanes do great damage to property, very few human lives are lost.

WORDS YOU SHOULD KNOW

alphabetical (al • fa • BET • ik • uhl) — arranged by letter in the order of the alphabet

atmosphere (AT • muss • feer) — the air that surrounds the Earth

category (KAT • uh • goh • ree) — a group

classified (KLASS • ih • fyd) — sorted into groups

committee (kuh • MIH • tee) — a group of people who perform a special task

condenses (kon • DEN • sihs) — changes from a vapor or gas into a liquid

cumulonimbus clouds (KYU • myu • loh • NIM • buhss KLOWDS) — a cloud formation with peaks at the top

cumulus clouds (KYU • myu • luhss KLOWDS) — a stack of clouds — round at the top and flat on the bottom

damage (DAM • ij) — harm; injury

device (dih • VYSS) — a machine or gadget

emergency (ee • MUR • jen • see) — a time of sudden need

enormous (ee • NOR • muss) — very, very large

equator (ee • KWAY • tuhr) — an imaginary line around the middle of the Earth

evaporate (ee • VAP • oh • rayt) — to change from a liquid into vapor

hemisphere (HEM • iss • feer) — half of the Earth's surface

molecule (MOL • ih • kyool) — the smallest particle into which a substance can be divided

meteorologist (MEET • ee • uhr • AHL • uh • jist) — a scientist who studies weather

severe (suh • VEER) — harsh; serious

storm surge (STORM surj) — a sudden rush of tidal waves

surround (suh • ROWND) — make a circle around

tropical (TROP • ik • uhl) — having to do with the warm regions of the Earth near the equator

violent (VY • oh • lint) — acting with great force

INDEX

About the Author

Arlene Erlbach has written more than a dozen books for young people in many genres including fiction and nonfiction.

She has a master's degree in special education. In addition to being an author of children's books, she is a learning disabilities teacher at Gray School in Chicago, Illinois. Arlene loves to encourage children to write and is in charge of her school's Young Author's program.